W9-ATG-366

"… on the first of January, in the year of our Lord one thousand eight hundred and sixty-three, all persons held as slaves within any State or designated part of a State, the people whereof shall then be in rebellion against the United States, shall be then, thenceforward, and forever free…"

— THE EMANCIPATION PROCLAMATION

THE EMANCIPATION PROCLAMATION

BY CHARLES W. CAREY, JR.

The Child's World®

GRAPHIC DESIGN
Robert E. Bonaker / Graphic Design & Consulting Co.

PROJECT COORDINATOR
James R. Rothaus / James R. Rothaus & Associates

EDITORIAL DIRECTION
Elizabeth Sirimarco Budd

COVER PHOTO
The Emancipation Proclamation / ©David Budd Photography

Library of Congress Cataloging-in-Publication Data
Carey, Charles W.
The Emancipation Proclamation / by Charles W. Carey, Jr.
p. cm.
Summary: Discusses the reasons for Lincoln's Emancipation
Proclamation and its impact on the institution of
slavery and on the course of the Civil War.
ISBN 1-56766-620-5 (library : reinforced : alk. paper)

1. United States. President (1861-1865 : Lincoln).
Emancipation Proclamation — Juvenile literature. 2. Lincoln,
Abraham, 1809-1865 — Juvenile literature. 3. Slaves —
Emancipation — United States — Juvenile literature. 4. United
States — Politics and government — 1861-1865 — Juvenile
literature.
[1. Emancipation Proclamation. 2. United States —History —
Civil War, 1861-1865. 3. Slavery — History] I. Title

E453.C37 1999
973.7'14 — dc21   99-19260
[B]   CIP

Contents

Did Lincoln Free the Slaves?

Most people know that President Abraham Lincoln freed American *slaves*. Not everyone knows that he did not free all of them. Lincoln was president during a difficult period in U.S. history. People in the southern states lived very differently from people in the northern states. For one thing, southerners owned slaves. Many northerners thought this was wrong. Over time, differences between the two parts of the country became serious. The South *seceded* from the rest of the United States. Soon, the nation was at war. This was the beginning of the *American Civil War*.

One year after the war began, President Lincoln decided to free some of the slaves. He hoped this would help the northern states, or the *Union,* win the war. In the end, Lincoln's decision led to freedom for all *African American* slaves in the United States. This is the story of how it happened.

More than 200 years ago, slaves lived in every American state. Slavery never became an important part of life in the North, but things were different in the southern states. Southerners became very dependent on slaves. Slavery gave white people the right to treat blacks differently. It allowed them to make blacks work without pay. Slavery also allowed whites to make their slaves work long hours under terrible conditions. The free labor the slaves provided helped southerners run *plantations*. These huge farms produced crops such as cotton and tobacco. Plantation owners earned a lot of money, and many were very rich.

CORBIS

SLAVES TEND THE CROPS ON A SOUTH CAROLINA PLANTATION. MANY SOUTHERNERS BELIEVED THEY COULD NOT SUPPORT THEIR FAMILIES WITHOUT THE FREE LABOR THAT SLAVES PROVIDED.

FREE STATES
BORDER STATES
SLAVE STATES

By 1861, most slave states had left the Union.
Delaware, Kentucky, Maryland, and Missouri
decided to fight for the Union, but these "border
states" still allowed their citizens to keep slaves.

By 1830, only three states had outlawed slavery: Massachusetts, New Hampshire, and Vermont. In each of the 21 other American states, slavery was still legal. Some Americans began to think slavery was wrong. Soon, *abolitionists* began working to end slavery across the nation. The Declaration of Independence stated that all men are created equal. Abolitionists believed this was true — not just for white people, but for blacks as well.

Most of America's slaves lived in the South. White southerners did not have to pay their slaves, so they could keep most of the money they earned. They also did not have to do the most difficult work — the slaves were expected to do it for them. White southerners did not want to give up the system of slavery. They believed that they could never run their farms without slaves.

Abolitionists in the North felt that slavery was cruel and unfair. Many northerners began to insist that the South end slavery. The southerners grew angry. Why were people in the North trying to tell them what to do? The southern states united. Then they threatened to secede from the United States. In 1861, that is exactly what 11 southern states did. The South became known as the *Confederate* States of America. By April 12, America was at war.

Four *slave states* stayed in the Union: Delaware, Maryland, Kentucky, and Missouri. These states were called *border states* because they sat on the border between the North and the South. Abolitionists wanted President Lincoln to free the slaves in these states after the war started. Lincoln refused. He knew the border states were important to the Union. Freeing the slaves might make the states' white citizens angry. Then they might choose to help the South.

Runaway slaves began to look to Union soldiers for help. Lincoln told the Union army and navy not to help the slaves escape. He wanted the South to come back into the Union as soon as possible. If he helped the slaves, that might never happen. In a letter to an army officer, Lincoln explained his thoughts. He wrote that freeing the slaves would "alarm our Southern Union friends, and turn them against us."

Lincoln knew that many soldiers were not fighting to free the slaves. Instead, they were fighting to put the United States back together again. Some Union soldiers did not believe the slaves should be freed at all. These soldiers might get angry if Lincoln helped the slaves. They might even leave the army! No matter how much the president wanted to help the slaves, there were many problems to consider.

In May of 1861, something happened that helped change the president's mind. It was a few weeks after the war had started. The Union army captured Fortress Monroe in Virginia. Three runaway slaves came to the fort. They asked the Union commander, General Benjamin Butler, if they could join his army. They wanted to fight against the South.

The *Fugitive Slave Act* had been in effect since 1850. It said that a runaway slave must be returned to his or her *master*. The owner of the slaves at Fortress Monroe came to see Butler. The man demanded that General Butler return the slaves. General Butler learned that the slaves had been forced to help build a Confederate fort. What if more southern slaves were used to help the South win the war?

General Butler made a decision. He said that the Fugitive Slave Law did not apply to these slaves. He said he would not return any slaves used to help the South. Instead, he told their master they were *contraband*. He refused to return the three men.

CORBIS

A GROUP OF FUGITIVE SLAVES ASKS A UNION SOLDIER FOR HELP.

Matthew Brady/Archive Photos

TWO AFRICAN AMERICAN SOLDIERS PREPARE FOR
BATTLE. THE UNION ARMY RECOGNIZED THAT ESCAPED
SLAVES COULD HELP MAKE THEIR FORCES STRONGER.

Lincoln was not happy with Butler's decision, but he did not try to change the general's mind. Before long, other slaves made their way to Union armies. Other generals refused to return the slaves to their masters. In fact, two Union generals fighting in the South decided to do even more. They began to free slaves in the areas that their armies controlled. Lincoln asked these two generals to return the slaves.

More and more escaped slaves were working for Union armies. Some U.S. congressmen began to think that slaves could help the Union win the war. Senator Charles Sumner, Senator Benjamin Wade, and Representative Thaddeus Stevens led the effort to let slaves join the war effort. All three men wanted to abolish slavery — both in the Confederate states and in the border states.

These leaders convinced the U.S. Congress to pass the first Confiscation Act in August 1861. This law said that any slave forced to build forts, haul supplies, or work for a Confederate army or navy was contraband. Under the Confiscation Act, Union soldiers could help such slaves run away.

In July 1862, Congress passed a second Confiscation Act. This law said that any slaves owned by Confederate soldiers, sailors, or government employees were contraband as well. Now Union troops could help these slaves escape, too. The act also gave Union generals permission to let runaway slaves join their armies.

Some Union generals encouraged large numbers of runaway slaves to join their armies. General Edward Wild, who fought in North Carolina, *recruited* enough runaway slaves to form a special unit. He called it "Wild's African Brigade." Soon, he began to send these brave soldiers to free other slaves in North Carolina.

The President Changes His Mind

Lincoln worried about the steps Congress and the generals had taken. He did not believe that the *Constitution* gave Congress the power to end slavery. He also feared that ending slavery would anger too many white people. Sometimes the battlefront was close to the border states. President Lincoln worried that people in these states might start helping the Confederates.

Lincoln could see that things had changed in the North. At first, northerners believed they were fighting to restore the United States. Lincoln had told them that was the purpose of the war. He had even said that slavery had little or nothing to do with the fighting. By the middle of 1862, many northerners supported the acts of Congress against slavery. They began to believe they really *were* fighting to end slavery.

CORBIS

PRESIDENT LINCOLN IS OFTEN CREDITED WITH FREEING AFRICAN AMERICAN SLAVES, BUT IT DID NOT HAPPEN QUICKLY. THE PRESIDENT HAD TO CONSIDER MANY THINGS BEFORE HE FINALLY TOOK ACTION.

Archive Photos

MEMBERS OF THE U.S. CONGRESS ASSEMBLE AT THE CAPITOL. DURING THE CIVIL WAR, CONGRESSMEN PASSED LAWS THAT ALLOWED UNION SOLDIERS TO HELP SOUTHERN SLAVES. LINCOLN WORRIED THAT SUCH DECISIONS WOULD ANGER MANY WHITE AMERICANS.

CORBIS

VIRGINIA CITIZENS OBSERVE THE USS *PENSACOLA*,
A UNION SHIP THAT PARTICIPATED IN THE BLOCKADE
OF CONFEDERATE PORTS.

Lincoln did not think these acts were a good idea. Still, he could see that many intelligent and important people supported them. He needed these people on his side to help the Union win the war. Lincoln decided to agree to all the acts against slavery.

Two European countries, Great Britain and France, were considering helping the South. These two nations bought most of their cotton from southern plantations. The Union navy had established a *blockade* that blocked the trade routes to the South. The blockade kept southern ships from transporting cotton to British and French mills. To help the South, the British began building ships for the Confederate navy. The French allowed Confederate ships to raid U.S. *merchant ships* docked in French ports.

What if France and Great Britain decided to do even more? What if they sent their navies to help the South? Together they could stop the Union blockade. Then the South might win the war. France and Great Britain also planned to give the South rifles, ammunition, and other supplies. This would help the Confederacy keep fighting. The war might drag on for so long that northerners would get tired and give up.

Lincoln knew that most citizens in Great Britain and France did not like slavery. Both countries had outlawed slavery many years before. What if he could convince the British and French that the war really *was* about ending slavery in the United States? The two nations would probably decide to stay out of the war. The North would not have to face such a strong opponent.

This left Lincoln with a big problem. How could he free the slaves in the South without angering the border states? After much thinking, he came up with an idea.

The Constitution gives the U.S. president some special powers to use only during a war. Lincoln decided to use his war powers to free the Confederate slaves. This would keep the South from using slaves to help them win the war. Slaves in the border states were not being used to help the South. That meant that Lincoln would not have to free them. Lincoln could tell the British, French, and the abolitionists that the North was battling slavery. At the same time, he would not anger the citizens of the border states.

Lincoln first told his *cabinet* about this plan on July 22, 1862. The cabinet members thought it was a good idea, too. William Seward was the *secretary of state*. He suggested that Lincoln wait to announce his idea until after the Union army won an important battle. Otherwise, people might think the president was using his plan only because he was afraid of losing the war. Lincoln agreed, and so he waited.

LINCOLN'S SECRETARY OF STATE, WILLIAM SEWARD, SUGGESTED THAT THE PRESIDENT WAIT TO ANNOUNCE HIS PLANS TO END SLAVERY IN THE SOUTH. HE BELIEVED IT WOULD BE BETTER TO WAIT UNTIL THE UNION WON A MAJOR BATTLE.

Archive Photos

GIDEON WELLES, Sec.of the Navy.   MONTGOMERY BLAIR, P.M.Genl   CALEB B. SMITH, Sec.of the Interior.
SALMON P. CHASE, Sec.of the Treasury.   EDWARD BATES, Atty. Genl
PRESIDENT LINCOLN.   WILLIAM H. SEWARD, Sec.of State.   EDWIN M. STANTON, Sec.of War.

PRESIDENT LINCOLN AND HIS CABINET.

IN COUNCIL, SEPT. 22ND 1862. ADOPTING THE EMANCIPATION PROCLAMATION, ISSUED JANY. 1ST 1863.

IN 1862, PRESIDENT LINCOLN DISCUSSED HIS IDEA
TO END SLAVERY IN THE SOUTH WITH HIS CABINET.
HE NEEDED ADVICE TO MAKE A DIFFICULT DECISION.

THE BATTLE OF ANTIETAM TOOK PLACE ON SEPTEMBER 17, 1862. IN A SINGLE DAY, BOTH THE CONFEDERATE AND UNION ARMIES LOST THOUSANDS OF SOLDIERS. IN THE END, THE UNION ARMY WON THE BATTLE.

He did not have to wait very long. In September, a Union soldier found some secret plans. He learned about a surprise attack the Confederates had planned. A Confederate army crossed the Potomac River into Maryland on September 17. They did not know that the Union army was waiting there. The battle became known as the Battle of Antietam (also known as the Battle of Sharpsburg). Although the fighting lasted only one day, it was the bloodiest battle of the Civil War. Both armies lost more than 10,000 men. Finally, the Union won the battle.

On September 22, Lincoln read the *Emancipation Proclamation* to the public. This presidential act would free any slave that was not living in the Union. It did not become law that day, however.

Lincoln said he would wait to sign it. He gave the South until January 1, 1863, to return to the Union. Then he would sign the Emancipation Proclamation. On that day, any slave in a Confederate state would be free.

The southerners had the Confederate army to protect them. They decided not to release any slaves unless the Union army marched in and forced them to. Millions of slaves continued to work in the South, just as they always had.

By January 1, only Tennessee had rejoined the Union. Lincoln signed the Emancipation Proclamation into law on January 1, 1863.

SLAVE OWNERS TRIED TO KEEP THEIR SLAVES FROM LEARNING ABOUT THE EMANCIPATION PROCLAMATION. STILL, THE WORD BEGAN TO SPREAD. SLAVES MADE PLANS TO ESCAPE TO THE NORTH WHERE THEY WOULD FINALLY BE FREE.

CORBIS/Bettmann

A Presidential Order

The Emancipation Proclamation is a short document. It is less than three pages in a modern-day book. Still, it is filled with many big words and difficult phrases. It is important to understand what the document says. First of all, *emancipation* is the act of making someone free. A *proclamation* is a formal public announcement.

The Emancipation Proclamation has three parts. In the first part, Lincoln reminds the Confederates that he warned them three months earlier to rejoin the Union by January 1, 1863. The document begins by saying:

Whereas, on the twenty-second day of September, in the year of our Lord one thousand eight hundred and sixty-two, a proclamation was issued by the President of the United States, containing, among other things, the following, to wit: "That on the first of January, in the year of our Lord one thousand eight hundred and sixty-three, all persons held as slaves within any State or designated part of a State, the people whereof shall then be in rebellion against the United States, shall be then, thenceforward, and forever free...."

In other words, the proclamation freed any slave living in a state that still chose to *rebel* against the United States.

THE EMANCIPATION PROCLAMATION MADE MANY PEOPLE ANGRY. SOUTHERNERS BELIEVED THAT PRESIDENT LINCOLN HAD NO RIGHT TO TELL THEM WHAT TO DO. MANY PEOPLE IN THE NORTH BELIEVED IT DID NOT DO ENOUGH TO END SLAVERY.

Archive Photos

EVEN AFTER THE EMANCIPATION PROCLAMATION, MANY SLAVES CONTINUED TO WORK AS THEY ALWAYS HAD. THEIR MASTERS REFUSED TO HONOR THE LAW OF PRESIDENT LINCOLN. MANY SLAVES WERE TOO AFRAID TO ESCAPE.

In the second part, Lincoln says which states must free their slaves. The Union army had run the Confederate army out of Tennessee. The North was now in control there, so Lincoln did not free any of its slaves. He also did not free all the slaves in Louisiana, because the Union army had invaded parts of that state in April 1861. In the areas where the Union had control, slaves were not set free. Lincoln freed only the slaves in Confederate areas of the state.

Lincoln also did not free all the slaves in Virginia. Like Louisiana, the Union troops had invaded only parts of that state. In Confederate areas of Virginia, the slaves were set free. Everywhere else, slaves were still considered to be the property of their masters.

Even after many battles, the Union still did not control any part of the other eight Confederate states. These states included Arkansas, Texas, Mississippi, Alabama, Florida, Georgia, South Carolina, and North Carolina. Because none of these states were under Union control, the Emancipation Proclamation went into effect — all slaves living in each of these states was now free.

The third part of the Emancipation Proclamation explains how the U.S. government would treat the freed slaves. It says that the Union military would protect them. They would make sure the freed African Americans were never returned to slavery. It also says that former slaves could join the Union army or navy.

This part of the document also discusses a serious problem. How would slaves survive if their masters did not give them food, shelter, and clothing? Lincoln did not have very much advice for the slaves. He said the slaves freed by his proclamation should keep working for their masters. He told them to insist that their masters pay them.

This was not a very practical idea. First of all, southerners did not believe that Lincoln had the power to free the slaves. They were not going to pay slaves to work just because the President of the United States said they should. After all, they had seceded from the United States. He was not even their president! Even more important, the main reason the Confederates were fighting the Union was to keep slavery. The freed slaves had two choices. They could run away to the North, or they could also stay in the South and continue living as slaves.

Many people were unhappy with the Emancipation Proclamation. Most Confederates hated it. Many northerners in the slave states did not like it, either. They feared the president might free their slaves next. Abolitionists were unhappy about the proclamation, too. They wanted Lincoln to free ALL the slaves, but that hadn't happened. Some people claimed that the Emancipation Proclamation achieved very little. It only freed slaves in places that the Union army did not control. Some people even made jokes about the proclamation. They said Lincoln freed all of the slaves he couldn't free, and none of the slaves that he could.

Still, most northerners were in favor of the Emancipation Proclamation. By 1863, most of them realized that the war was now about slavery. They also knew that unless slavery was abolished once and for all, they would never be able to live peacefully with southerners. Most northerners believed that Lincoln had dealt with the problem of slavery as well as he could at the time.

Of course, southern slaves were very happy about the proclamation. For the very first time, they could run away to a safe place. The North would no longer honor the Fugitive Slave Act. Thousands of slaves tried to escape as soon as they heard Lincoln had set them free.

A GROUP OF SLAVES MAKE THEIR WAY NORTH AFTER
THE SIGNING OF THE EMANCIPATION PROCLAMATION.

Imperial War Museum/Archive Photos

MORE THAN 600,000 SOLDIERS DIED DURING THE AMERICAN
CIVIL WAR. AS TIME PASSED, MANY NORTHERNERS SIMPLY
WANTED THE WAR TO END.

What Was Accomplished?

The Emancipation Proclamation was not perfect, but it did achieve many important things. First, it convinced northerners that soldiers were fighting not only to restore the United States, but to help the slaves, too. Many realized the war could make the United States a better place.

By 1863, many northerners were tired of the war. Thousands of Union soldiers had died fighting against the Confederates. The war was costing millions of dollars. The government needed a lot of money. Citizens of the North were paying higher taxes to help pay for the war. Northerners even began to think the Union should just let the southern states secede. Some people asked Lincoln to give up the proclamation. They hoped this might encourage the southern states to return. Lincoln refused. He said, "Should I do so, I should deserve to be damned through all eternity." President Lincoln was committed to helping African Americans.

Lincoln's proclamation made many northerners feel better about the war. More and more people realized that slavery was cruel and unfair. The war forced people to think about things that they once tried to ignore.

SOME PEOPLE ASKED PRESIDENT LINCOLN TO REVOKE THE EMANCIPATION PROCLAMATION, BUT HE REFUSED. LINCOLN BELIEVED ANY COUNTRY THAT ALLOWED SLAVERY COULD NEVER CLAIM TO BE FREE.

CORBIS

The proclamation also told the people of Great Britain and France that the United States intended to end slavery. This made the citizens of those two countries reconsider helping the Confederates. After the Emancipation Proclamation, Great Britain and France offered very little help to the Confederates.

The proclamation also allowed more than 200,000 blacks to join the Union forces. Nearly half of these blacks were runaway slaves from Confederate states. About 40,000 came from the four border states. They ran away to join the army even though they were not free. Some black soldiers came from the other Union states. Some even came from Canada. Many of these men had been born free. Others were slaves who had run away to the North many years before. Some joined the Union forces to help free their family and friends in the South.

One thing was for sure — the African American soldiers offered great help to the Union. The North was having trouble finding enough men to serve in the military. With the help of black soldiers as cooks and laborers, there were more soldiers to fight on the front lines. The Union also formed several units with only African American soldiers. These soldiers were known for their courage and bravery.

Eventually, the Emancipation Proclamation did help free all the slaves. Abolitionists worried about what would happen to the freed slaves after the war. The proclamation was only in effect during the war. Would black people be forced to return to slavery at the end of the war? Abolitionists wanted to make sure that this would never happen. They also wanted to free all the slaves who were not freed by the proclamation.

CORBIS

AFRICAN AMERICAN SAILORS WORKED ABOARD THE USS *Vermont*, A UNION NAVY SHIP. THE UNION FORCES EMPLOYED THOUSANDS OF FORMER SLAVES DURING THE CIVIL WAR.

CORBIS/Bettmann

GENERAL LEE, LEADER OF THE CONFEDERATE FORCES,
SURRENDERED ON APRIL 9, 1865. THE CIVIL WAR WAS
FINALLY OVER, AND THE NATION WAS REUNITED.

The abolitionists began working to change the Constitution. They planned to create an *amendment*. It would outlaw slavery everywhere in the United States. They spoke to government leaders about their plan. In 1864, Congress voted on the 13th Amendment — the amendment to end slavery. Unfortunately, it did not pass.

Lincoln was re-elected president later that year. Clearly, the North supported his decisions. He decided to work with the abolitionists. He hoped to convince enough congressmen to vote in favor of the amendment. Finally, it passed in February 1865. The amendment stated that slavery was illegal throughout the entire United States. If enough states agreed to it, the amendment would be added to the Constitution.

Lincoln was very pleased. Finally, something good had come from the war. More good news was to follow. On April 9, 1865, General Robert E. Lee of the Confederate army surrendered. The American Civil War was over, and the North had won.

Just five days later, President Lincoln was assassinated. He would never see the 13th Amendment become law. Later that year, many states agreed to the amendment. On December 18, 1865, Secretary of State Seward made an announcement. The 13th Amendment had been added to the Constitution. Slavery would be illegal in the United States forever.

WHEN THE CIVIL WAR ENDED, MILLIONS OF SOUTHERN SLAVES WERE FINALLY FREE.

CORBIS

Many people helped Abraham Lincoln create the Emancipation Proclamation — and ultimately to free the slaves. In fact, Lincoln himself said, "I claim not to have controlled events, but confess plainly the events have controlled me."

The Emancipation Proclamation paved the way for a nation of true freedom. Lincoln himself knew how important the document was. He said, "In giving freedom to the slave, we assure freedom for the free."

Even though President Lincoln is given the most credit for issuing the proclamation, there were many other people who worked to help African American slaves. Abolitionists, congressmen, generals, and even the slaves themselves played important roles in abolishing slavery. At the end of the Civil War, all Americans were finally free — just as the Declaration of Independence promised nearly a century before.

Archive Photos

LINCOLN NEVER LIVED TO SEE THE 13TH AMENDMENT BECOME PART OF THE CONSTITUTION. HE WAS KILLED ON APRIL 14, 1865 — JUST FIVE DAYS AFTER THE AMERICAN CIVIL WAR ENDED.

CORBIS

AFRICAN AMERICAN CITIZENS IN WASHINGTON, D.C., CELEBRATED THE
ABOLITION OF SLAVERY AFTER THE 13TH AMENDMENT BECAME LAW.

Timeline

1789	The Constitution makes slavery legal in the United States.
1830s	Abolitionists begin working to end slavery.
1861	Eleven slave states leave the Union in February. They form the Confederate States of America.
1861	General Benjamin Butler decides that runaway slaves are contraband. The first Confiscation Act is passed by Congress.
1862	The second Confiscation Act is passed by Congress. Lincoln tells his cabinet about his plan to free the slaves on July 22. Union generals free some slaves in Louisiana and North Carolina. The Battle of Antietam takes place on September 17.
1862	Lincoln reads the Emancipation Proclamation to the public for the first time on September 22. He tells the Confederates that he will sign the act and make it a law if they do not return to the Union.
1863	Lincoln signs the Emancipation Proclamation on January 1. Confederate slaves are free.
1864	Congress first votes on the 13th Amendment. It does not pass.
1865	Congress approves the 13th Amendment in February. The American Civil War ends on April 9. President Lincoln is assassinated on April 14. The 13th Amendment is made into law on December 18. Slavery becomes illegal in the United States.

Glossary

abolitionists
(ab-o-LISH-uh-nests)
Abolitionists were people who wanted to end slavery in the United States. The abolitionists did not believe that the Emancipation Proclamation helped enough slaves.

African American
(AF-ri-kan uh-MAYR-ih-kan)
An African American is a black American whose ancestors came from Africa. Slaves in the United States were African Americans.

amendment
(uh-MEND-ment)
An amendment is a formal change to the U.S. Constitution. The 13th amendment made slavery illegal throughout the United States.

American Civil War
(uh-MAYR-ih-kan SIV-el WAR)
The American Civil War was fought between the North and South. The war lasted for four years between 1861 and 1865.

blockade
(blok-AYD)
A blockade is a way of blocking an enemy so its people or vehicles cannot travel freely. The Union navy created a blockade with military ships to keep southern merchant ships from sailing.

border states
(BOAR-dur STAYTZ)
The border states were the slave states that stayed in the Union. These states separated the North from the South.

cabinet
(KAB–net)
A cabinet is a group of people who help the U.S. president make important decisions. President Lincoln read the Emancipation Proclamation to his cabinet on July 22, 1862.

Confederate
(kun-FED-uh-ret)
Confederate refers to the slave states (or the people who lived in those states) that left the Union in 1861. The Confederate States of America were also called the Confederacy.

Constitution
(kahn-ste-TOO-shen)
The Constitution is the basic set of laws for the United States. The nation's founders wrote the constitution in 1789.

contraband
(KON-tre-band)
Contraband is something that can be taken from its owner because it is illegal. During the American Civil War, African American slaves that escaped to the North were called contraband.

emancipation
(ee-man-se-PAY-shun)
Emancipation is the act of making someone free.

Fugitive Slave Act
(FYOO-jet-iv SLAYV AKT)
The Fugitive Slave Act was issued by the U.S. government in 1850. It stated that runaway slaves found in the North had to be returned to their masters.

Glossary

master
(MAS-ter)
A master is the owner of a slave.

merchant ship
(MUR-chent SHIP)
A merchant ship is one that carries items to be sold, such as food, clothing, or tools. Merchant ships are usually unarmed and cannot protect themselves against armies.

plantations
(plan-TAY-shenz)
Plantations are large farms (or several farms together) that grow crops. Before slavery was abolished in the United States, many plantations used slaves for free labor.

proclamation
(prok-le-MAY-shun)
A proclamation is a formal public announcement.

rebel
(ree–BELL)
If people rebel, they fight against their country's government. The Confederates rebelled against the United States.

recruit
(reh-KREWT)
If someone recruits others, he or she encourages them to join the military or other group. The Union army and navy recruited black men to join their forces.

secede
(sih–SEED)
If a person or thing secedes, it leaves someplace. The South seceded from the United States to form its own country.

secretary of state
(SE–kreh–tayr–ree of STAYT)
The secretary of state is the person who is in charge of the relations between the United States and other countries. William Seward was the Secretary of State during the American Civil War.

slaves
(SLAYVZ)
Slaves are people who are forced to work for others without pay. All slaves in the United States were finally free after the American Civil War.

slave states
(SLAYV STAYTZ)
The slave states were the American states where slavery was legal. The states in the South were all slave states.

Union
(YOON–yun)
The Union was all of the states that did not leave the United States during the American Civil War.

Index

For Further Information

Books

Hughes, Chris. *Antietam (Battlefields Across America).* Brookfield, CT: Millbrook Press, 1998.

Kent, Zachary. *The Civil War: A House Divided.* Springfield, NJ: Enslow Publishers, 1994.

Young, Robert. *The Emancipation Proclamation: Why Lincoln Really Freed the Slaves.* Minneapolis, MN: Dillon Press, 1994.

Web sites

The National Archives discussion of the Emancipation Proclamation:
http://www.nara.gov/exhall/featured-document/eman/emanproc.html

Lincoln and the Civil War:
http://debate.acusd.edu/~mdoms/page1.html

Visit the Library of Congress exhibit, "Mr. Lincoln's Virtual Library":
http://lcweb2.loc.gov/ammem/alhtml/alhome.html